MW01181075

A NEW WORLD OF SIMULATORS

TRAINING WITH TECHNOLOGY

CHRISTOPHER W. BAKER

NEW CENTURY TECHNOLOGY

THE MILLBROOK PRESS
BROOKFIELD, CONNECTICUT

Cover photograph courtesy of NASA

Photographs courtesy of I-Sim Corporation: pp. 1, 33; Multigen/Paradigm: pp. 4; Thomson Training & Simulation: pp. 6, 7, 11 (bottom), 29, 31; Partek Forest, Inc.: p. 9; Intersim and Rick House: p. 10; NASA Ames Research Center: pp. 12, 13, 16, 20, 21, 22, 24, 25, 27, 30, 35, 36, 38, 39; MicroWINGS.com: p. 18; DaimlerChrysler Corporation: p. 34; NADS at the University of Iowa: p. 40.

Published by The Millbrook Press, Inc.
2 Old New Milford Road
Brookfield, Connecticut 06804
www.millbrookpress.com

Library of Congress Cataloging-in-Publication Data
Baker, Christopher W.
A new world of simulators : training with technology / Christopher W. Baker.
p. cm. — (New century technology)
Includes index.
ISBN 0-7613-1352-4 (lib. bdg.)
1. Computer simulation—Juvenile literature. [1. Computer simulation. 2. Computers.
3. Virtual reality.] I. Title. II. Series.
QA76.9.C65   B35   2001
003'.3—dc21   00-056872

A NEW WORLD OF SIMULATORS

Fighter jets dive toward their target. The inset image shows the same view using infrared radiation instead of visible light.

Screaming through the air at 800 miles (1,287 kilometers) per hour, you see the treetops just 200 feet (61 meters) below your F-21 fighter jet as a solid blur. You top a rise and there, in the fog at the far end of the valley, lies your target. Your head-up display, flashing data across the inside of your helmet visor, shows your approach vector and wipes away the fog with a computer sleight of hand. The jet hugs the downhill slope, taking you to the valley floor. The target, bracketed on the display, draws closer. Soon it will be within range.

Suddenly a warning shrieks. Enemy radar has lit you up and is locking on for the kill. The contrail of a surface-to-air missile catches your eye as you take evasive action, pulling up hard and out of the valley. The missile closes in. You release the jet's countermeasures to knock it off track, but it stays with you. Up, down, wherever you move, its greater speed and maneuverability bring it racing up behind, leaving you only seconds to eject before your craft is blown to pieces.

A fighter jet diving into a simulated valley.

There was nothing else you could have done. Or was there? Heart pounding, you remove your helmet, climb out of the now-motionless cockpit, and head off to review the experience with your instructor. You have not just lost a 100-million-dollar aircraft. You are not downed behind enemy lines. You are a fighter pilot in training, using the latest multimillion-dollar simulator, preparing for a war that you hope will never come.

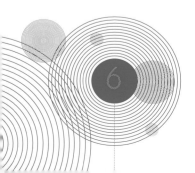

6

Before we answer this question, maybe we should first look at one of the primary uses for simulators—training. Whether we realize it or not, we have all trained to use any number of things, from the very simple, like a screwdriver or an apple peeler, to the more complex, like a lawn mower, a washing machine, or even a car.

Training, as you might have guessed, is just another way to say learning or teaching. Someone who trains you, teaches you. All of us have lots of trainers in our lives, from schoolteachers, to parents, to friends who know how to do something we would like to learn. As a simple example, let's say we don't know how to use a screwdriver yet. How would we go about getting that knowledge?

We could look in a book and get some ideas about what a screwdriver does, how to hold it, and how to turn a screw. To really learn to use a screwdriver, however, we would actually have to pick one up and practice with it. The best way to start is to find someone who is experienced with the tool and can show us how. For example, a father might show his son how he uses a screwdriver and then let him try it himself.

The father can guide the boy's hands, help him center the screwdriver on the screw head, show him how to hold the screw so it won't fall over, and demonstrate how much to push and turn the screw at the same time so it will enter the wood. It sounds easy, but

Here a soldier trains with the latest small arms in realistic battle conditions. Police departments around the country are also using similar systems to hone their officers' skills in dealing with dangerous situations.

depending on the learner's age, may take many tries to master well. And in the process the screwdriver could slip and scratch the boy's hand, gouge the wood the boy is working on, or even hurt the person working with him.

THAT'S AN EXPENSIVE SCREWDRIVER!

Now let's imagine another tool. This one, however, costs millions of dollars, possibly even billions, can destroy property worth millions of dollars, and kill or injure many people if used incorrectly. That's some kind of screwdriver! What could it be?

It could be a fighter jet like the one in the opening paragraphs of this book, or an oil supertanker loaded with millions of barrels of crude oil, or even a control tower at a busy airport trying to guide thousands of travelers safely into and out of a major city.

All these things are tools, too. They are just a great deal more complex than a simple screwdriver. And the consequences of using one of them in the wrong way are far more dangerous than a simple scratch on the hand. For example, if you were the captain of an oil tanker and hadn't learned that it can take many miles to bring your giant ship to a stop from full speed, you might not slow down soon enough to avoid a deadly reef by a harbor entrance. A crash could mean millions of barrels of oil coating beaches, killing animals and damaging the local ecology for years to come.

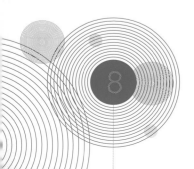

Using forestry equipment is hard and dangerous work. Here we see an operator learning to control the Partek Forest Harvester in the safety of a training simulator.

The bow of a ship, as seen from the ship's bridge, enters a fictitious harbor. This image was created to demonstrate a ship bridge-training system.

Similarly, the men and women who control nuclear-power plants, pilot commercial airliners, captain submarines, and direct other complex systems all need to be very well trained. With the proper training they can learn to operate their systems in the safest way possible and act with the best of knowledge in any given emergency.

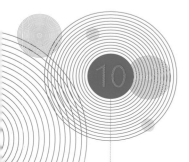

At this point, however, we can begin to see a real problem. How can people who do not know how to fly a jet or run a power plant learn to do it correctly without endangering themselves or the people around them? If they have to use a real power plant or passenger jet, a mistake could be disastrous. This is where simulators can help.

Simulators are systems that imitate other complex systems like submarines, space shuttles, airplanes, control towers and more, but do it all in a completely safe environment. Simulators are also used for other tasks like product testing or evaluation of scientific theory, both of which we will examine later. The primary task of simulators, however, and the reason they were originally invented, is for training.

Inside a simulator a mistake is something you can learn from. It is a place where you can experience the most dangerous of situations without worrying about the consequences. A commercial pilot can test what happens with a sudden change in cabin pressure at high altitude. A tank battle-group can practice maneuvers against an enemy under heavy fire. Or a power-plant operator can learn what to do if his or her nuclear plant is on the verge of a meltdown. Simulators allow all of this to happen without danger to people or property.

Simulators allow pilots to test-fly dangerous situations, like this near-miss accident, without danger to themselves, their passengers, or their plane.

Simulator systems are now sophisticated enough that groups of tanks, as shown below, can train together as a single battle group.

Some simulators imitate exactly what operators will see, feel, and hear when they are in a real-life situation. They are set up to seem so lifelike that the user's mind will actually be tricked into thinking that what is being experienced is the real thing.

We're on the runway and ready for takeoff inside a NASA flight simulator. Note the small transparent screen hanging from the top of the pilot's windshield. This is called a Heads-Up Display (HUD).

In commercial-jet flight simulators, for example, a pilot looking out his window at the start of a flight will see the jetway to the side. He will feel the initial jerk and push as the plane is backed away from the loading gate. And if it is snowing, he might even see the tracks of his plane's front wheels on the ground.

He will hear the engines rev higher as he throttles up to taxi and notice the slight sense of movement and the bumps in the uneven pavement of the airport taxiway. And finally, on take-off he will feel the increasing surge of acceleration as the plane speeds down the runway and launches itself into the air.

All of these elements—the sounds, the feel of the controls, the vibrations, the images seen through the windows—combine to create a lifelike experience. It seems like magic, but it is really a very complex set of interactions between hardware and software that make it all possible.

Before anyone could land on the Moon, astronauts had to spend countless hours practicing their landing skills. Here we see the Lunar Excursion Module (LEM) simulator executing a perfect landing.

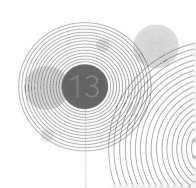

13

Simulating by Hand

There were several attempts to build flight simulators starting as early as 1910, but most were very simple and usually operated by hand. One was a half barrel placed round-side-down, with stubby wings sticking out the sides. A prospective pilot would sit in the barrel while others held the wing tips and moved them up and down. This would roll the craft side to side, and the operator would try to line up a movable bar with the horizon. As you can guess, such devices were not terribly effective.

In a sense, simulators have been around since the dawn of civilization. Some ancient ritual-combat practices might even be considered simulators of sorts, since they were created in part to teach young warriors certain aspects of attack and defense without endangering their lives. Certainly some of the devices used in medieval times to train knights for jousting tournaments could qualify as simulators.

One such device looked like the upper torso of a man with his arms outstretched. In one hand was a target. From the other hung a mace, a heavy, spiked, metal ball dangling from a chain. The trainee would ride forward and hit the target with his lance or sword. The force of the blow would spin the wooden man, swinging the mace around to attack the rider. If the rider ever forgot to duck he would be dealt a blow from the mace and possibly knocked out of his saddle. It was a grim, but not deadly, reminder of what a real-life opponent could do if you weren't always on your guard.

Training devices of all sorts have existed for centuries, but the modern era of simulators really only began in the years between World War I and World War II. It was during this time that Edwin Link built one of the earliest mechanically controlled flight simulators.

Edwin Link was an engineer who trained in his father's business, the Link Piano and Organ Factory in Binghamton, New York. It was in the basement of this factory that the younger Link built his first flight simulator, a stubby-winged box set on a series of bellows that normally provided air for the organs built at the factory. An electric suction pump sent air to the various bellows supporting the simulator, causing it to tilt and turn, depending on how the pilot moved the controls.

This first Link simulator was advertised as being both an aeronautical trainer and a profitable novelty device. This connection between training and entertainment still exists in the world of simulators today. Almost every major amusement park now has simulator rides that send park-goers into active, motion-filled adventures, using the same technologies employed in creating training simulators.

FLYING BLIND

Although they were a great step forward in training pilots, early flight simulators were still missing one key component: They had no instrumentation in the cockpit. Next time you happen to be on an airplane, look through the cockpit door as you enter or leave the plane. You will be amazed by the hundreds of dials, slider gauges, indicator lights, and toggle switches that cover every inch of the interior walls.

Some, like the altimeter, tell the pilot how high above sea level she is flying, others, like the compass, tell her in what direction the plane is heading, and still others tell her the angle of the plane's wings. All of these, plus many more, are necessary for safety, partic-

15

ularly if the plane must fly through fog or clouds, where visibility can be severely limited.

It was soon realized that effective flight training required instrument training as well. In the early 1930s the Link Flight School became one of the first to install the necessary gauges in their trainer, which had become known as the "Blue Box" because of its stubby look and bright blue color. To make sure that the pilot would focus solely on the instrumentation during his simulated flight, a hood that could be lowered over the new pilot's head was added to the trainer.

Once the pilot was enclosed inside, the simulator operator or instructor could then maneuver the Blue Box using the bellows controls. To keep his plane on course and under control, the pilot would then have to read the information on his instruments and adjust his controls according to what he saw.

The famous "Blue Box" designed by Edwin Link that trained countless World War II pilots to fly.

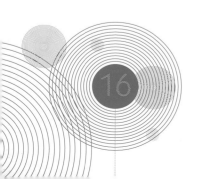

A Mechanical Tortoise

Shortly after instrumentation was added to simulators like the Link Trainer, a new device was developed to increase training levels. It ran on three wheels and looked somewhat like a small tortoise. The device was connected to the Link Simulator and moved slowly across a map on the instructor's table, depending on how the pilot inside the Blue Box moved the controls.

As the turtle moved, it left a line of ink on the map showing where the pilot was flying. This allowed the flight instructor to send signals to the simulator based on the plane's position along a specific flight path. For example, if the ink line showed the plane flying along a course that in the real world would bring it in contact with radio navigation beacons, the instructor could manually send those signals to the pilot inside the simulator, thus making the training flight more convincing.

The World War II Link simulator in action. The pilot is sitting in the cockpit with the top of the simulator open. The instructors are at a desk behind him, feeding information to his controls. Note the "turtle" device on the table crawling across the open chart.

Simulators at Home

As simulator hardware and software have become more affordable, an entire home-simulator industry has been born. The Internet is now host to regular flight-simulator tournaments and virtual grand prix road races. Home flight simulators run the gamut from a simple joystick connected to a standard PC, to elaborate home-built cockpits with realistic flight controls and windshield-mounted computer monitors. There are even affordable one-person motion platforms available that can give you full-motion, at-home adventures.

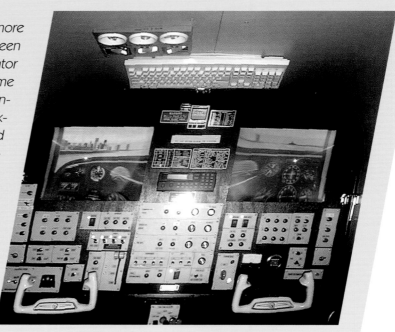

Homemade simulators can be used to fly or drive over the Internet. Here we see a home-built cockpit ready to fly at MicroWINGS.com with all the controls and visual systems in place.

THE ELEMENTS OF THE FUTURE

From our perspective the roots of modern simulators seem a long way away. The Blue Box looks like little more than a child's toy in which prospective pilots played "let's pretend." It is hard to imagine that hundreds of World War II fighter pilots trained successfully on such a primitive device.

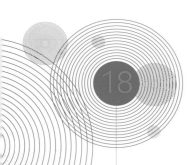

Today, however, the feeling of realism when a pilot climbs aboard a simulator is almost total. He enters a cabin that is identical to the plane he will actually fly. In fact, the cabin comes directly from the airplane manufacturer with everything from the leather seats to all the toggles and control levers in place. Furthermore, everything that the pilot sees, feels, or hears is designed to imitate reality as precisely as possible.

Just what is it, beyond the stage props of cabin and instrumentation, that makes a modern simulator seem so real? It is actually a combination of separate elements, from the motion platform on which the simulator cab sits, to the high-resolution visual system that presents the outside world through the windows, to the accurate responses from the controls and gauges.

And at the heart of this incredibly complex system lies the ever-present computer, without which current simulators could not exist. The computer is what ties the whole system together, interpreting the complex equations that define a plane's motion, creating accurate pictures of the surroundings, and providing instant feedback to any action taken by the simulator pilot.

LET'S GET MOVING

The first time you see a full-motion simulator, you will likely be struck by its insectlike appearance. It's not hard to envision it scuttling off

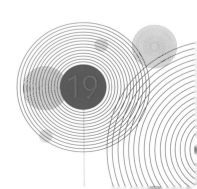

19

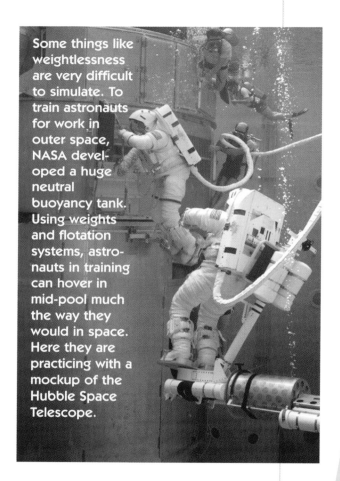

Some things like weightlessness are very difficult to simulate. To train astronauts for work in outer space, NASA developed a huge neutral buoyancy tank. Using weights and flotation systems, astronauts in training can hover in mid-pool much the way they would in space. Here they are practicing with a mockup of the Hubble Space Telescope.

It's More Than Just Digital

Most simulators now use the computer to control the created reality, but not all do. At NASA, for example, astronauts are trained in weightlessness using two physical systems—a large tank of water and a real airplane.

To use the float tank, astronauts are equipped with suits that look and behave very much the way their space suits would behave when in outer space. They are connected to air hoses and weighted so the astronaut will neither sink nor rise in the water. Surrounded by divers whose job is to respond in case of emergency as well as to manage the various hoses and tethers, the astronauts then practice some of the tasks they will have to perform in the weightlessness of space. These may include satellite maintenance procedures on life-size satellite models or activities inside the space shuttle bay.

While the float tank provides experiences that are very similar to weightlessness, and allows extensive periods of near-weightless training, NASA's air lab gives astronauts the real thing. In this case, the astronauts are carried aloft inside the fuselage of a large Stratotanker fuel carrier. Everything inside has been removed, and the walls of the fuselage are padded.

Once the plane reaches the desired altitude, it flies on a downward arc at the same speed that the people inside would fall if they were simply released in the air. Since the plane and the astronauts are falling at the same speed, inside the plane the people feel as if they were totally weightless and can "fly" around the open cabin. The only limitation is that since the plane is descending toward Earth, the length of weightlessness is usually not more than twenty seconds at a time.

into some dark corner on its spindly-looking hydraulic legs. These legs are, in fact, what provide the simulator's motion, but the feet never actually leave their spots on the ground.

The part of the simulator on which the cab or room on top sits is called the motion base or motion platform. All simulators that provide a physical sense of movement have motion bases, whether the simulator is used as an amusement park ride, a pilot trainer, or a trucker's training system.

The motion bases of advanced simulators provide movement with "six degrees of freedom." This means that the simulator cabs can move up and down, back and forth, and side to side.

Thus, when a pilot wants to bank the simulator plane and climb to higher altitude, the motion base turns, tilts, and moves upward. From the outside it looks like some crazy giant-insect dance, but to the pilot inside it feels exactly as if he were flying a real airplane. The amazing thing is that the simulator actually moves very little to create the feeling of motion. In fact, most commercial jet trainers have a range of motion in any of the six directions of less than 2 yards (1.8 meters). And in entertainment simulators the distance is smaller still, often only about 18 inches (46 centimeters).

Here we see a NASA 747 flight simulator in action, heading into what looks like a steep dive. The rounded part on the left is the projection screen, which wraps around the front part of the inner cabin. The angular section in back is where the pilots and the instructor sit.

Degrees of Freedom

The phrase "degrees of freedom" refers to the range of possible motions. If something has two degrees of freedom, it can move along a single line either forward or backward. This would be like a tightrope walker moving along her cable.

If, however, we say something has four degrees of freedom, this means it can move not only backward and forward but also side to side. This would be like a pencil drawing lines on a piece of paper. Since you can move the pencil in these four directions, there isn't a spot on the paper you can't reach.

Finally, if something has six degrees of freedom, it can move both back and forth and side to side as well as up and down. This would be like a housefly in a box. Since the housefly can move not only back and forth and side to side like the pencil, but can also move vertically, up and down, it can reach every spot inside the box. Thus, six degrees of freedom gives you full motion inside a three-dimensional space.

With six degrees of freedom, almost every possible movement of a jet fighter can be simulated.

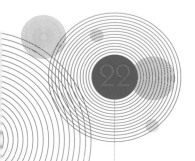

FOOLING THE BRAIN

In a real jet we can feel the acceleration for several minutes as we climb from the runway to 35,000 feet (10,668 meters). How is it possible, then, to get this same feeling inside a simulator that generally can move less than 3 feet (1 meter) in any direction? The trick lies within the brain of the person using the simulator, and involves stimulating all her senses at the same time so her brain believes that the simulator experience is real.

For those of you who have been to an amusement park and ridden on a simulator ride, think back to that experience. If you haven't yet done this, start your imagination and try to feel what it must be like. These rides often make you believe you are on a spaceship careening through the galaxy, or a runaway mining car racing along a track deep underground, or even a small submarine being chased by sea monsters. The wild twists and turns of the ride seem utterly real, but in fact they were all just make-believe.

The next time you sit inside one of these rides, close your eyes and block your ears. You will then begin to understand just how unreal they are. Without the sounds of the railcar, for example, clacking along its twist of track, or the sight of the steep dive ahead and the accelerating imagery sweeping past as you fall, you will simply feel the periodic jerking motions and vibrations of your seat.

If you concentrate on these sensations, you will notice that you never really move very far at all in any direction. What actually causes you to believe the ride is real is the coupling of these small movements with what you hear and see. Your ears hear the increasing rapidity of the clacking rails, your eyes see the gathering speed of the images whizzing past, and for a moment your body feels the move-

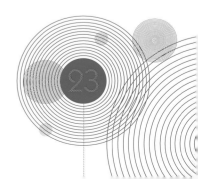

ment of the motion-platform. With all these intense sensations hitting the brain at once, your mind gets fooled into thinking something real is happening. The end result is that, even though the motion-base has exhausted its range of motion, you still feel as if you were hurtling ahead along the track.

This is exactly what happens to anyone using a full-motion training simulator, whether it is for jets, tanks, tanker ships, or trucks. The more realistic the sensory data is for all the senses, the more convincing the simulator will be.

SEEING IS BELIEVING

Looking out the window of a helicopter simulation on the NASA VMS simulator.

Now that you understand the importance of the insectlike motion-base, let's take a closer look at what goes on inside the cab above it. We have mentioned the interior of the cab itself, which is usually an exact replica of the system being simulated. Whether it's a helicopter, a truck, or an M-60 tank, the operator must be able to look around herself and see everything in exactly the same place as it would be in the actual system.

But what happens when she looks out the windows? Currently there are several approaches to displaying convincing visual imagery for simulators, from using television monitors or projection systems set in each window, to large movie screens and domes that surround the

NASA's Super Simulator

The biggest exception to the rule of simulator motion is the Vertical Motion Simulator (VMS) flight simulator at the NASA Ames Research Labs in California. There scientists and engineers have built the world's preeminent research system that can simulate several different types of flying craft, from fighter jets and rotorcrafts, to experimental design aircraft, the space shuttle, or even blimps.

There are six separate simulator cabs that can be converted into whatever aircraft the researchers are studying, and which can be transferred onto the motion-platform in less than a day. Furthermore, researchers from around the world can participate in the experiment without leaving their own labs by using NASA's Virtual Lab Internet connection.

Once the cab has been set in place, the fun begins. Besides being able to rotate, the cab can move as much as 60 feet (18 meters) vertically (as tall as a six-story building) in just a few seconds, 40 feet (12 meters) from side to side, and 8 feet (2.4 meters) from front to back. In addition, the cabs can be

A simulator in motion. In this time-lapse photo we see the dance of the VMS simulator.

To give you an idea of how far the NASA VMS simulator can move, here is a pair of shots with the simulator cab at the bottom and then the top of its 70-foot (21-meter) shaft.

faced in different directions to maximize the movement distance for a given test run. For example, an experiment may be set up to study how a rotorcraft, like a helicopter or a tilt-wing plane, drifts from side to side under heavy crosswind conditions. In this case, researchers might want to face the cab along the 8-foot (2.4-meter) line of motion, so they can use the 40-foot (12-meter) distance to study the sideways drift.

entire cab. Most often, the cab is set a few feet away from a large curved screen. The screen usually bends past the windows, so no matter how a trainee peers outside, she will see only simulated images.

The images are projected onto the screen from powerful projectors usually mounted on top of the cab itself. It is extremely impor-

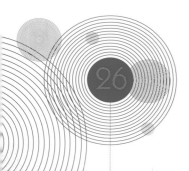

NASA's stunning FutureFlight center, an airport control tower simulator, features one of the most powerful simulators ever created. In this computer graphic representation you can see the surrounding screens with the image projectors outside the walls. The dark rectangles are mirrors that reflect the images from the projectors onto the various screens. This increases the distance the light travels, thus giving the image a true feeling of distance.

tant that the generated imagery be both accurate and created in real time. This means that the trainee should see what she expects to see and that if the craft is turned in any direction, imagery should change smoothly and evenly, just as in the real world.

Regardless of the mechanics of how the imagery is displayed, there is another aspect to the visual system that must be handled correctly if the imagery is to be convincing. To discover what it is, let's think about our eyes for a moment. First, sit at a desk and hold your index finger up close to your nose and look at it. Then move your finger out of the way and look at the far edge of the desk. And now, finally, take a look out a nearby window. Did you feel anything change as what you looked at changed?

What you felt was your eyes focusing and turning inward, depending on how close the thing you were looking at was to you. Now imagine what a pilot must see when he looks out his windshield. In a real flight nearly everything outside would be very far away, and the way his eyes focus helps to tell him that.

How are we going to provide that same sense of distance in the limited physical space of a simulator? After all, the screen is usually only a few feet away from the pilot's eyes. If the simulator pilot's eyes can notice this (and they will), then the trainee will sense that something is not quite real about his experience.

To remedy this problem, researchers use their knowledge that light from a distant source enters the eye in more or less parallel rays.

In a simulator, helicopter pilots can train for search and rescue before their help is urgently needed in the real world. Note how far away the landscape appears to them.

In other words, there is no noticeable point of origin from which these rays of light proceed. So, in order for long-distance imagery inside a simulator to look real, it must also appear to come from no specific point.

The solution is to somehow move the source of the imagery—the projector—far enough away from the screen that the convergence of the light rays is no longer noticeable. This can be done either by

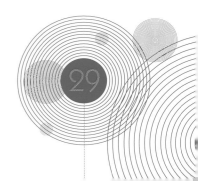

Engineers work on a giant model board for an early flight simulator. The track on the right holds the camera support allowing the pilot to "fly" over the model and practice landings on both a normal runway and an aircraft carrier just offshore.

Seeing into the Past

Real-time, computer-created imagery has freed the modern simulator of some of its greatest limitations. In the past even super-computers simply did not have the power to create images fast enough for most simu-lators, particularly flight simulators. For this reason a number of other approaches were used.

After the advent of television, TV tubes, model boards, and TV cameras were used to provide simulator imagery. First, an exten-sive miniature model of the landscape around a selected airport was created. This model, often 30 feet by 40 feet (9 meters by 12 meters) or more in size, was then set up on its side in a solid metal framework. A TV camera was then attached to a movable mount that could "fly" the camera into, away from, and all around the model board, depending on how the trainee moved the simulator controls. The images from the camera were shown on the TV tube mounted in the window of the simulator.

This was certainly an advance over having no imagery at all, but it was also severely limited. Since model boards were cumbersome and time-consuming to make, a pilot could usually only train using one or two models at most. Also, the camera, because of the size of the lens, could only come within a few inches of the model board itself. Coming any closer could, and often did, result in smashing the camera into part of the model.

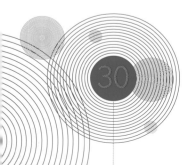

physically moving the projector or by somehow making the light travel a longer distance before hitting the screen and the viewer's eye.

The first approach sounds simpler, but it is impractical because of the typical size limitations of the simulator. The solution is to use a series of mirrors reflecting the light back and forth, thus increasing the length of its path before it reaches the viewer's eyes. The end result is a very realistic feeling of distance.

WHAT'S WITH ALL THE NOISE?

Think for a moment about the sounds that surround a tractor-trailer truck. At the start the door slams shut, the seat leather creaks, and the metal key ratchets into the ignition. In a simulator all of these sounds will occur if the cab itself is an accurate physical replica of a real truck.

But what happens in a simulator when the key is turned to start the engine? In a real truck the starter works for a moment, finally catching the big diesel engine, which awakens with its usual clattering roar. Truck-driving simulators, however, don't actually have engines in them. Where will the sound of the engine come from if the simulator cabs are just empty shells fitted with computer connections?

This is where simulated sound comes in. Just as the pilot needs to hear his jets rev up when he pushes the simulator's throttle, the trucker needs to hear the diesel engine start up when he turns the key. The coupling of this sound and a vibration from the motion platform

Training for driving a truck through the narrow streets of a European town, a truck driver gets not only a simulated view of the streets ahead, but can see what's behind in the rear view mirror.

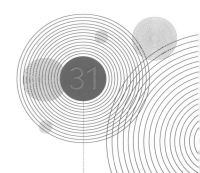

imitating the engine, along with the bumps of the pavement surface once the truck starts rolling, creates a very realistic experience. Similarly, in a flight simulator hearing the chatter from the other planes as well as communicating with a simulated control tower helps to complete the experience.

FEEDBACK FOREVER

The final major component of effective simulators, is not really a component you can point to at all. It is the feedback system. A trainee needs to see that the simulator is responding to her in the same way that the real system would. This means that the correct gauges in a flight simulator need to change, both when and how they would in the real world, in response to a pilot's action.

Not only must all the visible systems work together, but the simulator as a whole must exhibit the same behavior as the trainee would experience in a real situation. This means that not only the visuals, sounds, and motion must be as expected, but the physics of the simulator must mirror reality. Consequently, a pilot cannot be allowed to do a flip-turn in a Boeing 747 just by spinning the wheel. Or a trucker must not be able to shift from first gear to tenth gear, going zero to 60 miles (97 kilometers) per hour, at a single bound.

These sorts of basic physical limitations are encapsulated in a series of mathematical equations that accurately describe what is known about a given system's real-world behavior. The computers

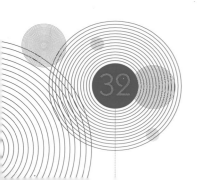

that run the simulator use these equations to guide its creation of realistic responses. Thus, if a pilot tries to bank her plane too sharply, the resistance in the controls will increase. And depending on how close to the plane's real performance limits the pilot is getting, the simulator could start shaking or vibrating in ominous ways, indicating a possible catastrophe about to happen.

Just-Enough Simulators

Every training requirement does not demand a thoroughly believable simulator experience to be effective. In fact, because of the high cost of top-end simulators, such an approach would be incredibly wasteful.

Ideally, in any training situation, what you really want is a simulator that only provides the necessary amount of information to train the user in the task at hand. For example, if someone is learning to drive a truck, one of the first tasks he needs to master is how to shift the complex transmission. To learn this, the prospective driver does not need to be immersed in the fully enclosed driving environment, which would be more useful for road safety training. He simply needs a system that imitates the shifting process.

For this reason, there are whole series of simulators that are much more task specific than the fully immersive kind. They may not be as impressive and exciting to look at, but they are equally effective.

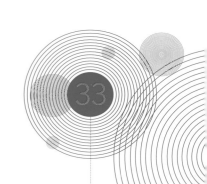

Dodge gives their RAM 1500 truck a workout. Car manufacturers use simulators that imitate all kinds of road conditions to "test drive" new models and ensure high quality.

Up to this point we have focused mainly on simulators used for training. However, simulators are used for several other very important purposes, including product testing and prototyping and scientific research.

Let's consider for a moment what it takes to design and build a new car, or even to introduce new control features to an existing model. As amazing as it may sound, a new car costs around a billion dollars to bring to market, even before the first car arrives in the showroom. This is a huge risk for any car manufacturer, and so to ensure that the risk pays off in sales, simulators are used at various stages in the development of new car models. In addition, car manufacturers need to be convinced that the various systems they install are safe.

Because of these concerns, most car manufacturers now use simulators for extensive testing during the design phase. Different kinds of simulators are used to test the various automobile components. For example, there might be a road-condition simulator to test the mechanics of a new suspension system or a virtual dashboard to provide designers with the look and feel of a new control or display system under development. Or, the auto company might utilize a fully immersive simulator through which engineers and designers can directly experience just how the car as a whole will behave in snow, rain, or almost any driving conditions.

For most of its relatively short existence the science of simulating reality has struggled to develop ways to evoke real-life experiences. In the early days flight simulators like the Blue Box were all tuned by hand. This meant that it was up to the flight instructor to decide which machine settings made the simulator "feel right."

With this "by feel" approach, simulator experiences were close enough to reality to be useful for a trainee. However, they were not precise enough to be useful as experimental tools themselves. Since each simulator potentially could be tuned differently by any given instructor, the precision required for scientific experimentation was missing.

Exacting scientific experiments only became possible after digital computers began to be powerful enough to

Simulating the wind in one of NASA's giant wind tunnels allows scientists to test resistance and drag on anything from a Humvee military vehicle to a full scale F-18 fighter.

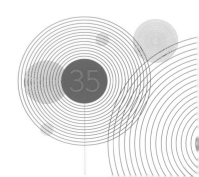

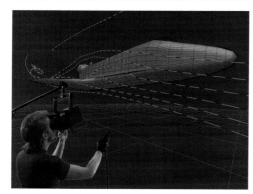

VR and simulators converge as researchers use virtual reality technology to take the place of simulator testing. VR is also useful for viewing data that have been gathered using real-world simulators.

Virtual Reality vs. Simulators: Is There a Difference?

Actually, the fields of virtual reality (VR) and simulators are growing ever closer all the time. Each uses the computer to present a convincing "other world" to our senses, and both are used for training, entertainment, and scientific exploration.

Perhaps the best way to distinguish between the two is to look at what they are used for. Simulators most often imitate real-life systems. Even the scientific experiments involving simulators are most often seeking to understand and improve real-world situations, such as driving safety or airport efficiency.

Virtual reality, on the other hand is more open-ended. In VR there are often no props, such as aircraft cabins or automobile bodies, because the computer usually generates the entire reality. For this reason VR hardware is often different from simulator hardware, favoring head-mounted displays and fiber-optic gloves over exact replicas of various machines.

In addition, VR is often used to study more abstract ideas, such as molecular structures or the birth and death of stars and galaxies. Over time, however, as computers become more powerful, it is likely that these two forms of simulating reality will converge. From the vantage point of today, it seems unlikely that you'll ever pilot a flight simulator through a black hole; but then again, sometime in the future that may be the best and safest way to study one of the universe's most mysterious entities.

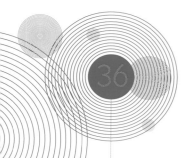

create very close and repeatable imitations of reality in the simulator. This did not occur until the late 1980s and early 1990s. Since then, as computers have increased in speed and sophistication so has the ability of scientists to use simulators to test theories about real-life situations.

NASA, for example, has developed two such simulators, the VMS system mentioned earlier and the FutureFlight central airport control tower. FutureFlight is an exact replica of a typical airport control tower and offers a 360-degree view of a simulated airport complete with aircraft taking off and landing, supply and fuel trucks servicing the planes, and readily changeable airports and weather conditions.

Using this $10 million cybertower, scientists plan to study air- and ground-traffic problems that lead to travel delays and accidents, as well as to train air-traffic controllers in a hyperrealistic setting. The overall goal is to make future travel safer and more efficient for us all.

Beyond this, the system can also be used to study layout and expansion plans in existing airports around the world. This information could help these airports handle the expected increase in air traffic over the coming decades. At San Francisco International Airport, for example, development plans call for adding a new runway to eliminate fog delays at the airport that plague winter flight schedules and to reduce noise. With FutureFlight, scientists can work with various design options to see which will be the safest before the airport decides on any course of action.

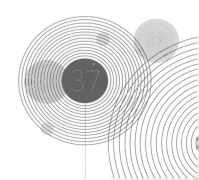

Facing page: While air traffic issues are the main focus of NASA's control tower simulator, the simulator is also being used to train shuttle launch staff. In addition, scientists studying the images returned by the Mars Pathfinder (left) can get a 360 degree view of the landing site.

Besides NASA simulators, universities around the country are using simulators and virtual environments to study real-world problems ranging from the design of safer industrial machines like metal stampers to the creation of more efficient farming machinery.

One such effort is the National Advanced Driving Simulator (NADS), currently under construction at the University of Iowa, which will be used to study advanced problems in traffic and driving safety. The system will allow scientists to simulate any sort of traffic situation, which can then be used to examine driver psychology and related responses.

39

A computer representation of the National Advanced Driving Simulator at the University of Iowa. This new facility will be the most sophisticated driving simulator in the world. Drivers will be able to experience complex, realistic driving scenarios as researchers study driver psychology, safety issues, and more.

Since these studies will all take place within the safety of the simulator, even dangerous accident scenarios, impossible to test in the real world, can be explored. Scientists will be looking to determine what sorts of new technologies, such as advanced vehicle communications, navigation systems, and control devices, will increase safety and efficiency on the highways of the future.

SIMULATING THE FUTURE

In truth the age of simulators has only just begun. Computers continue to grow exponentially in power. Thus their ability to create ever-more lifelike realities is increasing as well. In addition, scientists are continually discovering more about how to capture aspects of reality in mathematics and so be able to reconstruct those new insights inside a simulator.

Coupled with this is the continuing drop in price of the essential elements that make up a simulator. Peering only a short distance into the future, one can easily see that many may first learn to drive on a simulator. We can see the beginnings of this in the many road-racing arcade games. Each new generation of these games provides ever-more realistic experiences.

It is also likely that home and educational simulators will offer whole new ways for people to relate to one another over the Internet, not only through sports like auto and air racing, which is already pos-

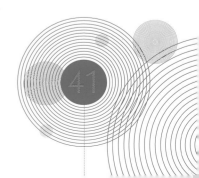

NASA's Transonic wind tunnel can deliver winds moving faster than the speed of sound. At right, we see the vanes that decrease tunnel turbulence and direct the winds, and, above, the giant fans that drive them.

sible, but in ways we can hardly imagine today. Will simulated tours of Paris let you feel the stairs on the long climb to the top of the Eiffel Tower? Will you smell the bread baking as you walk the virtual streets of Rome? Or will you be able to transport yourself back to 1789 to experience life at the start of the French Revolution?

It is possible nowadays to discern the beginnings of many such uses for simulators. How many will actually become part of our world is not known. One thing is certain, however—that simulators will play an ever-increasing role in helping us understand our world and make it a safer place to live.

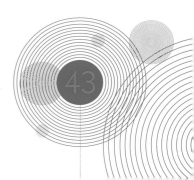

Try a search with any of the major Internet search engines using the keywords:

Simulators
Training Simulators
Driving Simulators
Flight Simulators
Golf Simulators
Education simulators

This will provide a list of hundreds of cool sites to visit. In addition, some of the best research and corporate simulator pages are listed below. Many contain tons of links to get you further into the subject. Have fun!

NASA Ames Research Simulation Laboratories
www.simlabs.arc.nasa.gov

NASA FutureFlight Central
surface.arc.nasa.gov/ffc

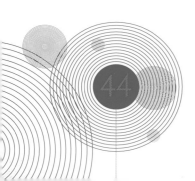

Thomson Training & Simulations
www.tts.thomson-csf.com

I-Sim corporation
www.i-sim.com

Other Simulator Links:

Driving Simulators
The French National Institute for Transport and Safety Research
www.inrets.fr/ur/sara/pg_simus_e.html

Home Flight Simulators Magazine
www.microwings.com

Training Systems and Simulators
electron.aero.swri.edu/tsd

Web-Based Surgical Simulators and Medical Education Tools
synaptic.mvc.mcc.ac.uk/simulators.html

Bodyflight Skydive Simulators
www.bodyflight.com

INDEX

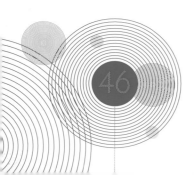

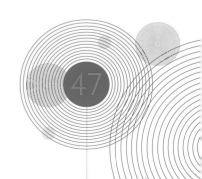

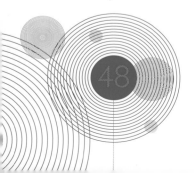